Lewis and Clark
A Journey of Discovery

© "Lewis and Clark in the Bitterroots" by John Clymer, Courtesy of Mrs. John F. Clymer and The Clymer Museum of Art.

By Emily Costello

CELEBRATION PRESS

Pearson Learning Group

Contents

An Adventure Begins

Can you imagine what life was like in the United States more than 200 years ago? There were no cars or airplanes and few roads. There were no electric lights or telephones. Just about every U.S. citizen lived east of the Mississippi River!

This is what life was like when Thomas Jefferson was the president of the United States. President Jefferson had many talents and interests. He was an educator, an **architect**, an inventor, a writer, and a musician. Most important, Thomas Jefferson was a patriot. He loved his country and was always thinking of ways to make it a better place.

Jefferson thought one way to help the United States grow and prosper was to extend its land west of the Mississippi River. So in 1803 he convinced the U.S. government to buy more than 830,000 square miles of western lands from France for $15,000,000. This land, called the **Louisiana Purchase**, stretched from the Mississippi River to the Rocky Mountains, and from the Gulf of Mexico to Canada. Few people in the United States knew anything about this land.

Jefferson wanted to know everything about this western land. He wanted to know about the geography, climate, plants, and animals. He wondered about the customs and languages of the Native Americans who **inhabited** this land.

Also, Jefferson hoped to find a Northwest Passage or water route linking the Atlantic Ocean to the Pacific Ocean. A water passage would provide a good **trade route**. So he decided to send an **expedition** into this wilderness to find the answers to his questions.

The Louisiana Purchase doubled the size of the United States in 1803.

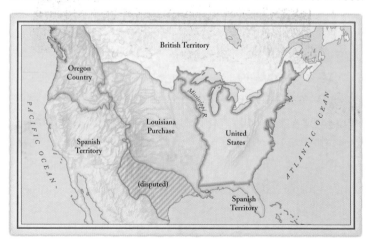

4

Meriwether Lewis   William Clark

To lead the expedition, Jefferson chose his trusted assistant, 28-year-old Meriwether Lewis. As a boy, Lewis had spent long hours exploring and learning about woodland plants and animals. Before working for Jefferson, he had been a captain in the army and was a doctor. As his co-leader, Lewis picked his friend and fellow army captain, 32-year-old William Clark.

The two friends headed for St. Louis, Missouri, where they recruited more than 40 men for their Corps of Discovery. Then, on May 14, 1804, the Corps set off for what would become one of history's greatest adventure stories.

Up the Missouri River

In his journal, William Clark sketched and described a bird he saw on the Plains.

The Corps traveled northwest up the Missouri River in a 55-foot-long **keelboat** and two smaller boats called **pirogues**. From the first day of their trip, many of the men, including Lewis and Clark, kept detailed journals.

The men's first days on the river were tough. It rained. Mosquitoes bit them. Their muscles were sore from paddling against a strong current. Each day they traveled only about 14 miles, going farther and farther into the wilderness.

Fun Fact

How much food might you need for a 3-year trip? For starters, Lewis and Clark took along 600 pounds of grease, 50 kegs of pork, 193 pounds of dried soup, 7 barrels of salt, and almost 2 tons of flour!

Luckily, the men were used to hard work. Before joining the expedition, many had been gunsmiths, **blacksmiths**, carpenters, and soldiers. Many of them knew how to survive in the wilderness, and they weren't afraid of venturing into the wild western lands.

Traveling with the group was York, an African American man who had been Clark's companion since childhood. Lewis brought his huge Newfoundland dog, Seaman. At first, Lewis and Clark had some discipline problems with the men. A few stole supplies. One fell asleep on guard duty. Another talked back to an officer. Two men **deserted**.

On August 20, 1804, Sergeant Charles Floyd died after a sudden illness. Historians say he may have suffered from a burst appendix. Floyd was the first U.S. soldier to die west of the Mississippi River and the only person to die on the expedition. The hilltop where Floyd is buried is now part of Sioux City, Iowa.

By autumn, Lewis and Clark reported no more problems, and it seems that the Corps began to work as a team. Perhaps they knew they had to depend on and trust one another as they moved into wilder territory.

President Jefferson had requested that the Corps meet as many Native American groups as possible, but they didn't meet any until late July. Then, while out hunting, a Corps member met a horseman from a group known as the Missouri. This led to a meeting with chiefs of the Missouri and another group known as the Oto.

Lewis and Clark tried to impress the chiefs. They showed off their magnets and compasses. They gave the chiefs and warriors gifts of beads, cloth, "peace medals," and more. The chiefs were polite and talked of friendship and trade. The Corps was allowed to travel peacefully through their land.

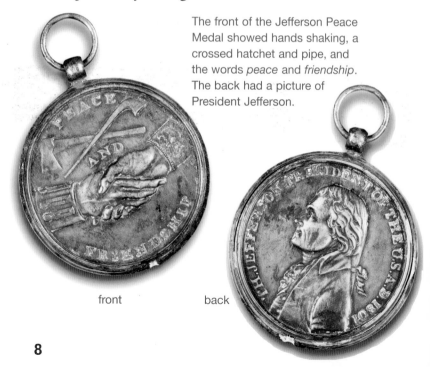

The front of the Jefferson Peace Medal showed hands shaking, a crossed hatchet and pipe, and the words *peace* and *friendship*. The back had a picture of President Jefferson.

front   back

Farther upriver, however, the Corps met the fierce Teton Sioux. The Corps had left their one member who spoke Sioux with another group of Sioux. Now there was no one to translate. The groups could not understand each other. When warriors tried to seize Lewis's canoe, Clark drew his sword in anger. The Sioux raised their bows. A fight was about to start!

A chief named Black Buffalo stepped in. He knew that the Corps had better weapons than his warriors, so he told the Corps to go on. Clark agreed, and a battle was avoided.

In late October, the group safely reached some friendly Mandan and Hidatsa villages near the mouth of the Knife River. About 4,500 people lived there—more people than lived in Washington, D.C., at the time! Lewis and Clark decided to build a fort and spend the winter.

While there, Lewis and Clark met and hired a fur trader named Toussaint Charbonneau as a translator to travel with them. With him would be Sacagawea, his young Shoshone wife, who had been kidnapped years earlier by the Hidatsas. She would be going back to her homeland in the west, so the Corps hoped she would help to guide them and talk to the Shoshone.

Farther West

Although the Mandans and Hidatsas had welcomed the explorers warmly, the winter was anything but warm. Some mornings the temperature dropped to 40 degrees below zero!

The long, bitter winter tested Lewis's skills as a doctor. He treated ax wounds and fevers. He had to **amputate** the frostbitten toes of a young boy. He helped Sacagawea give birth to a baby boy named Jean Baptiste. Clark later nicknamed him "Pompy" because the baby's funny actions seemed to be **pompous**.

The Mandans lived in earthlodges like this one.

The Mandan and Hidatsa villages were the last marked point on the explorers' map of the Missouri River. Lewis and Clark spent the winter quizzing the people about what lay to the west. The Mandans weren't much help as they didn't travel. The Hidatsas could tell them only about the land up to the mountains that are now known as the Rockies.

In turn, the Mandans and Hidatsas were curious about the Corps. For example, they were fascinated by York. He was the first African American man they'd ever seen. They considered him powerful and gave him the nickname Big Medicine because of his dark skin.

In March of 1805, the ice on the river began to break up. On April 7, the Corps were finally able to continue their journey west. The men continued to be amazed at the abundant wildlife. They stared at bighorn sheep, bald eagles, and cranes. The sound of beavers smacking their tails against the water kept them up at night. Six-hundred-pound grizzly bears chased them up trees, across the prairie, and into the river. The frightened men began to travel in pairs and sleep with their guns beside them.

In early June, the expedition came to a fork in the river. Both Lewis and Clark thought the clearer southern fork would continue to lead them westward.

The Hidatsas hadn't mentioned the fork, but they had told the travelers about a great waterfall. Scouting ahead, Lewis heard a roar. He saw what looked like columns of smoke rising from the river. He'd found the Great Falls of the Missouri, in what is present-day Montana.

In his journal, Lewis called the majestic waterfall on the Missouri River "the grandest sight I ever beheld." He soon found four more waterfalls farther upriver. The men had to **portage**, or carry their boats, more than 18 miles to get around the falls. It took the men nearly a month.

The Great Falls of the Missouri were too rough and wild for the Corps to travel by canoe.

An engraving done after the expedition shows a Corp member escaping a grizzly bear by climbing a tree. People who lived in the East had never seen a grizzly bear.

Animal Discoveries

President Jefferson wanted Lewis and Clark to make notes about the plants and animals of the West. They did an exceptional job. In all, they recorded 178 plants and 122 animals that were unknown to people who lived in the East. They saw coyotes, antelope, and bighorn sheep. They recorded (and tasted) steelhead and cutthroat trout. They spent a day capturing a prairie dog to study it. They were amazed at the sight of enormous herds of buffalo, and they had terrifying encounters with grizzly bears.

grizzly bear

Into the Land of the Shoshone

Lewis found the source of the Missouri River in the Rocky Mountains.

Finally, in late July, Sacagawea began to see landmarks she remembered. She told the others they were nearing the source of the Missouri River and the home of her people, the Shoshones.

Excited, Lewis scouted ahead. From a high point, he expected to see another river flowing west toward the Pacific Ocean. He was disappointed—all he saw were more mountains. President Jefferson had sent the Corps west to find the Northwest Passage. Lewis had failed to find it.

To reach the Pacific, the Corps would have to cross rugged mountains. Lewis now knew the Shoshones were vital to their success. The Shoshone had horses, and the Corps needed them to cross the mountains.

When Lewis first approached the Shoshones, the Native Americans were suspicious. The men of the Corps were the first white men they'd ever seen. Then Sacagawea came forward to translate and recognized the Shoshone chief. He was her brother, Cameahwait! He quickly promised to sell the Corps all the horses they would need.

On September 11, the Corps along with Sacagawea set off into the Bitterroot Mountains. Leading them was a Shoshone guide named Old Toby. The crossing was supposed to take about four or five days, but Old Toby lost the trail. Food ran low. It snowed, and still the mountains stretched out before them. The group was half-starved when they struggled out of the Bitterroots 11 days later.

Fun Fact

Sacagawea helped the Corps just by traveling with them. Native Americans thought a woman, especially one with a baby, meant the group was friendly. She was called "a token of peace."

Luckily, the Corps had wandered into the lands of prosperous Native Americans. They called themselves the Nimipu or "the people." However, Clark incorrectly translated their hand signals as "pierced nose" and called them the Nez Percé.

The Nez Percé gave the travelers salmon and roots to eat, and a place to rest. A chief named Twisted Hair showed them how to hollow out pine trees with fire and make new canoes.

By early October, the Clearwater River was finally behind them. The Corps were canoeing down the Snake River toward the Pacific Ocean.

The Nez Percé were still making and using dugout canoes when this picture was taken in 1910.

The members of the Corps were so anxious to reach the Pacific that they began to take risks. Instead of carrying the canoes around the rocky **rapids** of the Snake River, they shot through them, losing supplies in the rough water.

On October 16, the explorers' canoes reached the Columbia River. Crowds of Yakima and Wanapam people greeted them. In his journal, Clark made notes about these new groups who lived in houses made from woven fiber mats.

At the Columbia River, the Corps were far beyond the limits of the Louisiana Purchase and the U.S. border. They were slowly moving back into mapped territory. In 1792, a British explorer had traveled up the Columbia River from the Pacific Ocean. He'd seen and named Mount Hood in what is now the state of Oregon. Clark saw Mount Hood in the distance on October 18. It was proof that they were nearing the ocean.

The river now widened. Magnificent trees surrounded them. On November 7, Clark excitedly wrote, "Ocean in view! O! the joy." Actually, the Corps was still 20 miles from the sea. Storms, high water, and winds would prevent them from reaching it for another three weeks.

When they reached the ocean at last, Lewis and Clark had to decide where they would spend the upcoming winter. They asked the Corps to vote. Each person's choice was written down.

Together, the Corps agreed to cross to the south side of the Columbia River, near what is now Astoria, Oregon. There they would build their winter quarters.

Clark recorded in his journal that 554 days had elapsed and 4,132 miles had been traveled since they left Missouri.

Lewis sketched a eulachon, a small and oily marine fish that the Corps enjoyed eating during the winter.

The Corps' second winter was wet and miserable near the ocean.

Heading Home

You can still see Clark's signature on Pompey's Pillar, a rock he named "Pompy's Tower" for Sacagawea's son.

The winter on the Pacific coast was miserable and rainy. Finally, as their food supply dwindled, the Corps gratefully headed for home on March 23, 1806.

They reached the Nez Percé in May, but they couldn't cross the Bitterroots because there was still too much snow. In June, they finally were able to cross the mountains.

Now the group split into two so they could explore more of the land. Clark took a group down the Yellowstone River. Lewis headed up the Marias River.

Clark's group rode back to where they had left their canoes. Then several men took the boats down river toward Great Falls. Sacagawea led Clark and the rest of the party overland.

Lewis's return trip was less peaceful. On the way back to find Clark, Lewis and his men stopped for the night. As they slept, eight Blackfoot warriors tried to steal their horses and guns. A fight broke out. One Corps member stabbed a warrior. Lewis shot another. The six remaining Blackfoot fled the scene. Lewis and the men left the area quickly. They met safely with Clark and his group on August 12.

This map shows the trail the Corps of Discovery traveled.

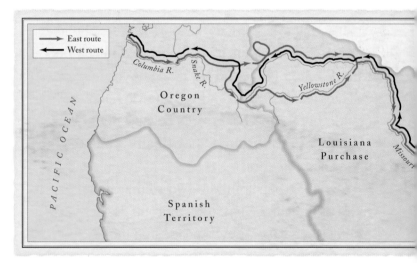

In mid-August, the Corps said goodbye to Charbonneau, Sacagawea, and Pompy. Another Corps member also left to become a fur trader.

Going east, the Corps now had the Missouri River's powerful current working for them. They covered up to 70 miles a day. Before long, they began to meet boats traveling the other way. Fur traders were pushing west. One of the traders told the explorers that many people thought they were dead.

Lewis and Clark reached St. Louis on September 23. They had been gone for nearly two and one-half years. The townspeople gave them a tremendous welcome.

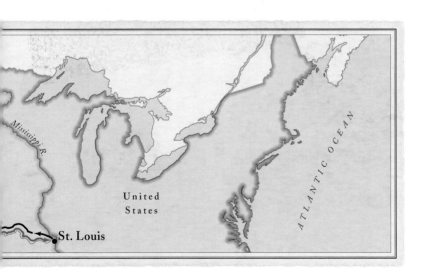

The End of the Trail

Once they had returned to the East Coast, Clark hurried off to Virginia to propose to the woman who would soon become his wife. Meanwhile, Lewis spent three months in the White House telling President Jefferson all about the Corps' journey.

Jefferson considered the trip a huge success. He was pleased with the maps, plant samples, and drawings the Corps brought back. He was grateful to learn more about the Native Americans who lived in the West. He didn't seem to mind that Lewis and Clark had failed to find an easy trade route to the West Coast.

Many statues have been built to honor Lewis and Clark.

Congress gave Lewis and Clark each 1,600 acres of land. The rest of the men received 320 acres each. Everyone received double pay. Lewis later became the governor of the Louisiana Territory, and Clark began a fur trade business. He also became governor of the Missouri Territory.

After the first excitement and celebrations of the Corps' return, the nation barely noticed the adventures and discoveries of Lewis and Clark. Lewis never prepared the pair's journals for publication. They were first prepared for printing by Clark in 1814, five years after Lewis died.

The lands Lewis and Clark explored weren't unknown to the rest of the United States for long. By the end of the century, ten states had formed along the route they had traveled, and nearly 16 million Americans had traveled from the East to settle the new lands.

People still admire Lewis and Clark because they wanted to travel into unknown lands just to find out what was there. They were brave, smart, and lucky enough to return. Through their descriptions and sketches of what they saw, we can have some idea of what our country was like so long ago and what it was like to live an adventure.

Glossary

amputate to cut off, especially by surgery

architect a person who designs buildings

blacksmiths people who heat and shape iron

deserted abandoned one's duty or job

expedition a journey taken for a reason, or a group who takes such a journey

inhabited lived in

keelboat a large, shallow boat used for carrying freight

Louisiana Purchase a large tract of land purchased from the French government by President Jefferson in 1803 that more than doubled the size of the United States. It extended from the Mississippi River to the Rocky Mountains, and from the Gulf of Mexico to Canada.

pirogues canoe-shaped boats

pompous self-important behavior

portage to carry boats and supplies overland from one lake or river to another

rapids parts of a river or stream where the water moves very quickly, often over rocks

trade route a pathway or road used to carry goods for sale from one place to another